CW00500161

THEIR LUNAR LANGUAGE

Charlotte Eichler was born in Hertfordshire in 1982 and now lives in Yorkshire. She has an MA in Norse and Viking Studies and works as a bibliographer at the University of Leeds. Her poetry has been published in numerous magazines and anthologies, including *PN Review*, *The Rialto* and *Stand*. Find her on Twitter @CLEichler.

Their Lunar Language

Charlotte Eichler

VP

Valley Press

First published in 2018 by Valley Press
Woodend, The Crescent, Scarborough, YO11 2PW
www.valleypressuk.com

ISBN 978-1-908853-98-1
Cat. no. VP0115

A CIP record for this book is available from the British Library.

Cover illustration by Felicity Hall.
Text design by Jamie McGarry.
Edited by Wendy Pratt.

Contents

Divination 9
The Coffin Calendars 10
Survivors 11
Trapping Moths With My Father 12
The Navigator 13
Balloonist 14
David 15
Halfway to Voronezh 16
Clean White Bones 17
A Pheasant 18
What Little Girls Are Made Of 19
At Mirror Lake 20
The Fifty-Year Traffic Jam 21
Owlish 22
Into the Fjords 23
Kaktovik 24
Fata Morgana 25
Last Egg Collection 26
Islomane 27
Hervör and Völund 28
Valkyrie 29

Acknowledgements

Many thanks to the editors of the following publications in which some of these poems first appeared: *Agenda*, *Blackbox Manifold*, *The Interpreter's House*, *PN Review*, *Stand*, *Strix*, *The Rialto*, *The Emma Press Anthology of Aunts*, *In Transit: Poems about Travel*, and *Best New British and Irish Poets 2017*.

I am very grateful to Jen Campbell and Vahni Capildeo for their advice, kindness and support, and to the *Poetry London* mentoring scheme. Thanks to Antony Dunn, Helen Mort, Peter Stark, Geraldine Rennison, Char March and Leeds Writers' Circle for their generous feedback and encouragement. Many thanks also to Wendy Pratt and Jamie McGarry at Valley Press, and Felicity Hall for her beautiful cover art. And, most of all, love and thanks to Ricky, Bill, Mark, Marie and my parents.

for Grampy and Moo Moo

Divination

We knew everything, playing oracle on the carpet.
Saturdays crawled with our ladybird circus –
from the ends of our fingers, solemn as blood,
    we sent them to find our future husbands.
We let them trickle down
    our wrists into the birdbath
to see if they'd keep walking while we drowned them,
jealous of their easy flight

    from one shape to the next.
Now, like hanged men, we want to buy futures
and there's someone doing tarot at the end of Brighton Pier.
    Stars are poking holes in the sky.
        There's an airy clatter

    of cards falling into place
but stranger things are happening beneath our feet:
coppers chink through the boards
    onto rows of starlings
stacking themselves like decks, noisy as a masked ball.
    We think *fluke* has something to do with wings
then remember whales, gliding
        despite the weight of all they know.
We watch the stragglers find their place under the pier,
    all the sea's dark spread ahead of us.

The Coffin Calendars

Miss June is given lilies, Miss December's in white fur. In the woods, twelve walnut caskets for us to stand in. Childhood Sundays, the moth-eyed rows of old men, half-living. *Memento mori* paintings hanging on the walls, the angels in the aisles with noseless shadows. My smile says too much about my skull. I try to stay still – the photographer says next year we'll all have guns and camouflage bikinis. In town, people turn their heads as far as owls do. Our dresses show the winged blades of our backs as we fly off the shelves – and the men, the men joke they can't see the coffins.

Survivors

Aunts drink tea for hours – they have no mirrors or clocks
but each other's faces tell the time.

Why do their hands shake and rattle the cups in their saucers?
We prowl the flat – the hallway dark with years of coats,

the dining room with carpets on the walls.
Each visit we think something will be different

but there's always the same red View-Master
with unchanging views of Prague, and no TV.

We draw elaborate tunnels and hold funerals for bees;
the cheese plant grows towards the window.

Our aunts show us a glass case of curled-up figures.
All we want is the china cockatoo and toy koalas.

Their arms come towards us lined with numbers –
we wriggle away from their touch.

Trapping Moths With My Father

You come to life as you name them:

swallow-tailed

twenty-plumed

spectacled

camouflaged by day, like you.

Endlessly arriving on our beams of light

dust-soft

drifts of them

printing the white sheet.

Our heads lean close in this midnight silver

and our breath
curls together in the cold.

Look closer:
their dark wings are inscribed

with eyes and feathers,

hieroglyphs you understand but can't explain.

They speak a lunar language

and are trying to get back.

The Navigator

Your hands don't look like yours,
the skin dough-pale and grazed.
I think of how we used to walk on walls
holding onto those huge thumbs,
even the narrow black railings by the river,
one foot in front of the other

faster and faster.
You were so used to fear –
swallowing it quick like scalding tea
in the mess, battling fog
over the world shrunk to a map –
we thought it was invisible to you,

although later you remember
where the graze came from:
walking home with us you'd dragged
your hand along the wall until it bled
to keep you conscious
so we wouldn't be afraid.

Balloonist

Haworth Gala, 1906

She is wet to the waist
in river, a minnow girl
slipping through lanes,
always looking
for the ropes

somebody hangs
in the woods
near water,
or that feeling you get
at the edge of cliffs.

On the moors
the walls lose
their footing,
lurching up hills,
along scars.

She looks down on the village,
pictures it wilder –
black hats a penguin circus,
the Old White Lion
roaring her name –

all those extra hearts
to bloody her.
She chooses
the balloon's silky bones,
a lampfish sky.

David

Six foot five and all you eat:
a single bowl of mackerel
and a one-inch square of bread
to ‘toast the Queen’.

Coming from a bath,
your body’s brittle coral,
your spine
a seahorse curve.

We wish we could see

your blue heart
through the pane
of your skin

because you never
answer questions,

flicking light
from yourself

like a shoal.

Halfway to Voronezh

On a stopped train,
sharing the chocolates
your fiancée gave you
for the journey,
trying not to giggle
as two men gut fish
on the table below,
our carriage filled
with blood and sea.
The stations we pass
look temporary,
concrete platforms
without signs.
An unreal place
that doesn't count.
When the heating breaks,
it only makes sense
to share warmth.
The train pulls into the city
and before you leave
we get coffee,
watching twelve brides
round a statue, posing
in varying shades of white.

Clean White Bones

Two cuttlefish are waving
in their glassy world
as I go to hold your hand.
Our fingers clash

and I wonder
if it's any easier for them,
with twenty legs to tangle,
six hearts to please.

They speak a patterned language
of moody stripes and flashes,
the signs of love imprinted
on their skin,

leave their eggs
like a dropped necklace,
ruffled versions of themselves
suspended in each blackened bead.

I shift and break our grasp,
thinking of the jewel you offered,
of all their hearts
and our half-hearted kisses.

If we could take their place
there'd be no mess,
just our children in the weeds
brightening like bulbs.

A Pheasant

Beside us, copper tail cocked –
Aladdin's lamp.

What Little Girls Are Made Of

I.

A green itch:
she pinches little wings
then plucks a leg.
A glass bead grows in its place,
the way some weeds she picks
confess white sap.
More cluster round a rose:
she is making lines of limbless flies.
Ants leave a trickle of red
down her thigh.

II.

She peels shells from flowerpots,
waits till they unfurl
and presses each cool body
to her skin. Her mother calls –
she leaves with snails
suckered to her legs like kisses.

At Mirror Lake

It took us by surprise, how fast the moon rose –
a stone thrown from the cliff

floating loose in hot blue sky.
We asked why, as if its grey bloom

in the day was extraordinary.
Our words clipped, unkind with fatigue.

I watched your profile – the suddenly unfamiliar
curve of your nose. We thought we knew

how things like day and night
and love would work.

I held you too hard, my nails
made chilly little moons along your arm.

The Fifty-Year Traffic Jam

sits tyre deep in sphagnum moss
surrounded by cracked glass
and rusting fern.

In spring, blue tits
hurl themselves at wing mirrors

and oily pools collect electric dragonflies
with copper wire wings.

The forest drinks them in,
sucks up radiator fluid
and cogs –

its creaking branches
sound more metallic
by the day.

Owlish

Promised an owl, we wait hours
picking over the indigestible
parts of our day –
needle-fine bones,
soft fur dropped at our feet.

I'm nested in your jacket's down,
winged by your arms,
half in the place where trees
smoke into cloud.

Into the Fjords

Someone's turned over
a mirror, the grey-backed sea
a polished image of the sky.

Waterfalls pour upwards,
meeting themselves at the shore –
windows in pieces on the water,
sills waving –

whole villages submerged and shimmering.

Clouds hide a wreck,
a ship's broken ribs, splintered

like this edge of land – leaning over
the bow, I see myself
capsized.

Kaktovik

We hear it singing songs of solid ice.

Our children dance in dirty sandals

on the slick black head of a whale,

the islands by our town   all eyes.

We share out red insides,
braise sourdock and blubber,
press round the warmth of cigarettes.

Winter comes anyway –

the snow sprouts claws,

pads through the streets after dark,

cracks its teeth on the bones we left behind.

By the icehouse, a mother
licks new colours from her fur,

far from her blue world

and the cub that melted as they swam.

Our homes are barred with shovels, antlered –
she's close enough to taste the glass.

At night, wind flutes through the whalebones –

Fata Morgana

Water has caught this place –

rivers split and trap houses
so they're swimming next to barnacled cars
as cod leap up to line roofs.

Salt crusts everything – the grass crackles with it.

Kittiwakes nest on the windowsills
painted red to match their tongues
and girls' hair is brown and shiny as seaweed –

their boats hover
just above the harbour.

Everything made of unreachable light.

Last Egg Collection

From here the sea
between stacks
is a green ribbon –

thick socks
and a horsehair plait
stop us plunging

down rock
white with seabirds,
laced with nets.

We fight the sword-beaks of gannets
for our snowy harvest
of eggs and feathers.

Below,
the empty houses
look like open graves.

Islomane

'Islomania – a rare but by no means unknown affliction of spirit. There are people … who find islands somehow irresistible. These born "islomanes" … are direct descendants of the Atlanteans.'
– Lawrence Durrell, *Reflections on a Marine Venus* (1953)

She thinks of unhatched things:
eider weaving slippery nests
from the surf,

sharp rains
of skua and tern
when she strays from the path.

Some days she misses people
and sees them in the seals
strung out in lines beyond the breaking waves.

With a toe in the water,
she leaves rows of pleated shells –
wedding dresses

and the trees filling
with a robin's twisted
ribbons of song.

Hervör and Völund

I held the birds of myself together
for seven years.
When I left with his ring,
he made seven hundred

to tempt me back.
Offered earrings like green eyes,
brooches of milk teeth,
silver cups like small skulls.

I put our sky-blue eggs
beyond his reach,
up where distance
softened everything to feathers.

I loved his hands,
their blacksmith skill.
He loved black velvet bark
after a fire.

But it wasn't only metal he could shape.
Now he's far above me,
a vulture with black fingers
and a blood-drop head.

Our children's veins were green-lit –
young trees
with the smell of smoke
already in their branches.

Valkyrie

Swans settle down to sleep among the cabbages,
wings touching like the paper dolls
she strings across her door.

She watches from the window,
thinks of all the words she knows for dark.
Tonight, she goes to them –

they croak to each other, their bright beaks,
the bow curves of their necks.

She looks back to her house
and her arms feather in the cold.

Lightning Source UK Ltd.
Milton Keynes UK
UKHW04f1334150818
327267UK00003B/80/P

9 781908 853981